John Cottingham is Professor Emeritus of Philosophy at
the University of Reading, Professor of Philosophy of
Religion at the University of Roehampton and Honorary
Fellow of St John's College, Oxford. His many books
include *The Spiritual Dimension*, *Philosophy of Religion:
Towards a More Humane Approach*, *Why Believe?* and
How to Believe.

Little Books of Guidance

Finding answers to life's big questions!

Also in the series:

HOW CAN
I BELIEVE?

A little book of guidance

JOHN COTTINGHAM

First published in Great Britain in 2018

Society for Promoting Christian Knowledge
36 Causton Street
London SW1P 4ST
www.spck.org.uk

The author and publisher have made every effort to ensure that the external
website and email addresses included in this book are correct and up to date
at the time of going to press. The author and publisher are not responsible
for the content, quality or continuing accessibility of the sites.

Scripture quotations are in some cases taken from the AV or the NIV and in
other cases use the author's own phrasing.

Extracts from the Authorized Version of the Bible (The King James Bible),
the rights in which are vested in the Crown, are reproduced by permission of
the Crown's Patentee, Cambridge University Press.

Scripture quotations taken from the Holy Bible, New International Version
(Anglicized edition). Copyright © 1979, 1984, 2011 by Biblica (formerly
International Bible Society). Used by permission of Hodder & Stoughton
Publishers, an Hachette UK company. All rights reserved.
'NIV' is a registered trademark of Biblica (formerly International Bible
Society).
UK trademark number 1448790.

British Library Cataloguing-in-Publication Data
A catalogue record for this book is available from the British Library

ISBN 978–0–281–07691–8
eBook ISBN 978–0–281–07692–5

Typeset by Manila Typesetting Company
First printed in Great Britain by Ashford Colour Press
Subsequently digitally reprinted in Great Britain

eBook by Manila Typesetting Company

Produced on paper from sustainable forests

Contents

1

The starting point

But my dear Sebastian, you can't seriously believe it all.
(Evelyn Waugh[1])

The challenge that the sceptical Charles Ryder puts to his friend Sebastian in Evelyn Waugh's *Brideshead Revisited* sums up an attitude that has become steadily more dominant in our contemporary culture. Over the last few generations we seem to have seen a steady shift from a world in which religious belief of some kind was the 'default' position for the majority, to one where it is an option only for a diminishing minority.[2]

This applies, of course, to the developed Western world. There are many parts of Africa, the Middle East and Asia where religion remains central to the lives of most people, and shows no signs of losing its hold. So the sceptical and detached attitude of Charles Ryder is by no means the norm in the world as a whole, though it has become fairly typical of our own Western culture.

Is the decline of religious faith in the West something to be regretted? It partly depends on which aspects of religion you're considering. A religion-dominated society can be an environment where intolerance and bigotry reign and fear and oppression flourish. Many Westerners

1

pride themselves on their humane values, but one does not have to go back many generations to find a time when Christians in Europe were burning other Christians to death for their beliefs.

So there are aspects of religion that the modern Western world may be grateful to have left behind. But rather than go over that old territory, let us start our inquiry with a rather different and more directly personal question. Are we – are *you*, the reader – completely comfortable with living entirely without religious faith?

It's perhaps not easy to answer that question with complete honesty. But when the jaded Western tourist looks out from a hotel window in Amman or Marrakesh and hears the strange haunting wail of the call to prayer floating over the city in the clear morning light, he or she may feel a sneaking pang of admiration for a culture where each day still begins with the praise of God. The mess and the grime of another day will soon be unleashed, but here is a timeless moment of affirmation, a brief space set aside to acknowledge the utter dependency of humanity on a power it cannot fully understand but which it has felt a deep need, since time immemorial, to acknowledge.

A similar pang of nostalgia may grip the visitor to Jerusalem as the shops and offices fall silent on Friday evening and the sabbath lamps are lit. None of the difficulty or anguish of human life has disappeared, but here is a brief pause in which secular time gives way to sacred time, a time of renewal and reflection, following a custom passed on down the generations in faith and hope that human life has a deeper significance than the utilitarian imperatives of work and survival.

And even in disillusioned and disbelieving north-western Europe there are still cities where on Sunday morning the bells ring as they have done for hundreds of years calling the people to worship, and where the churches still receive those who have come to start another week by taking stock of their lives, offering up their anxieties and hopes, and singing out their hymns of prayer and praise, not expecting or demanding magical good luck or miraculous solutions to their problems, but as a simple act of duty and thanksgiving and affirmation.

A sentimentalized vision? Perhaps to some extent it is. But it may succeed in bringing home the idea that religious belief is not just a matter of giving assent to certain doctrines, or finding certain credal teachings intellectually plausible. Religion is integrally bound up with *praxis* – with patterns of action and behaviour and observance that are integrated into the daily and weekly routines of life in ways that confer structure and bestow significance.

Our lives, to be sure, are punctuated by many routines – routines of work and of leisure, of eating and sleeping, of family concerns and business transactions. But the structures and practices of religion are different in kind from any of these. Those who engage in them feel, perhaps not always but at least on some occasions, that they glimpse a deeper meaning and purpose to their lives. At its best, religious observance seems to afford a brief respite from the relentless grind of secular activity, a fragile window into a region that is hard to define or explain, but which something in us recognizes as having a special kind of significance – the region of the sacred.

You do not have to be a committed believer to recognize this elusive and precious dimension of our human existence. One of the fiercest contemporary critics of religious belief has recently conceded that there is such a thing as 'spiritual experience', and that it can be among the most 'important and transformative' occurrences in our lives.[3] And another prominent self-styled 'materialist' and representative of the 'new atheism' is on record as acknowledging a 'numinous' and 'transcendent' aspect to our lives, which is 'beyond the material or not entirely consistent with it'.[4]

It remains to be seen how we are to come to terms with this 'numinous' or 'sacred' or 'spiritual' dimension. But a more general point about the framework for our inquiry may perhaps already have emerged from these opening remarks. When people ask 'Should I believe?' or 'How can I believe?', it is often assumed that what is wanted is an intellectual inquiry into the truth of religious claims, or an analysis of the evidence or arguments that support religious belief. This calls to mind the detached, sceptical standpoint of Charles Ryder in our opening epigraph – 'How can you possibly *believe* all that?' But while there is nothing wrong with approaching religion via analysis and scrutiny of the relevant beliefs and doctrines, this is not the only way to tackle the subject – not even the only philosophically respectable way. There is another way: to start by thinking not about the doctrines but about the practices and observances that give religion its shape, and the heightened human experience (of the sacred, the spiritual, the numinous, or whatever term we use) that nourishes it. If we focus on these things, then perhaps the question 'How can I believe?' will end up answering itself.

2

Why want to believe in the first place?

> You want to cure yourself of unbelief and you ask for the
> remedy.   (Blaise Pascal[1])

Some people, perhaps with pain and effort, have thrown off what they now regard as the illusory religious beliefs of their childhood, and they may be angry or irritated if anyone suggests they should reconsider. Others, particularly among the younger generation of educated Westerners, may have had little if any direct childhood contact with religious belief and may possibly be curious about what it involves and whether they themselves could ever be drawn to become believers. Yet another group, perhaps because of crises or setbacks in their lives, may find themselves thinking wistfully about what it would be like if they could ever embrace the comforts and consolations of being a believer.

But what exactly are these supposed comforts and consolations? More broadly, what could *motivate* someone to want to become a believer in the first place? For unless there is some motivation, some initial wish or inchoate inclination to open up the question of religious belief as at least a conceivable option, then the question 'How can I believe?' could scarcely get off the ground.

When people speak of the 'consolations' of religion, they may well be thinking of belief in the afterlife. This is identified by many as the key component of being a religious believer; hence one quite often hears remarks like, 'I'm not religious – I think that when you die, that's the end.' Blaise Pascal, in the seventeenth century, who was one of the first to raise the question of how one might motivate oneself to become a believer, laid great stress on our hopes or fears regarding the eternal happiness or misery that awaited us in the next world.[2]

Yet Pascal's emphasis is by no means the only possible one. A great deal of religious belief and practice is, and always has been, concerned with a deep sense that our lives need redemption, that we need to turn aside from our selfish and wasteful pursuits and seek a more fulfilled and abundant life here and now. The goal, in the words of the Gospel, is 'that ye might have life, and have it more abundantly'.[3]

There are, no doubt, many aspects to this richer and more 'abundant' existence, but one of them is that religious belief typically appears to confer a sense of *meaning* to life. It would be absurd to say that an atheist's life cannot contain many worthwhile and meaningful activities. But for the religious believer, human life is typically seen as having an additional significance that is the key to its ultimate meaning – what might be called a *cosmic* significance.

The best way to see what this involves is to set it against the opposite view. If the modern scientific-materialist conception of the cosmos represents the final truth, then human life, together with love, consciousness and all that we value and treasure, is the result of inexorable physical laws operating blindly, without plan or purpose. It is of no more ultimate significance than an evanescent vapour that coalesces on a planetary rock for a while, as long as certain chemical configurations happen to arise, but is destined sooner or later to vanish, just as the rock itself will vanish, engulfed by the dying embers of the star around which it revolves.

Perhaps, by resolutely pursuing our own chosen activities and projects, we can salvage what meaning we can from this terrifyingly blank and indifferent cosmic backdrop. But however we construe it, our human existence will still be no more than a strange cosmic excrescence appearing and then disappearing without any more ultimate point or purpose than any of the other relentlessly unfolding events – shifting of tectonic plates, collisions of meteors, explosions of supernovas, spinning of galaxies – that mark the slow and inevitable running down of the universe towards the final stasis of total entropy.

Suppose, by contrast, that the core idea of traditional theism is true – the idea that at the heart of things is a living divine presence that is the source of all being and goodness. In that case, then, our human existence, even granted that it arose out of the long chain of forces and reactions described by science, will nevertheless be more than just an accidental byproduct of those inexorable physical processes. It will be ultimately *grounded* in something that gives it meaning and purpose. Our human nature, however often we go astray and turn towards darkness and despair, will nevertheless be fundamentally ordered towards the good – towards a purpose not of our own devising that is intrinsically good, and in which alone our true fulfilment is to be found.

It is this kind of vision, this sense of ultimate 'groundedness', that led the great twentieth-century philosopher Ludwig Wittgenstein to speak of a religious outlook as involving the feeling of being 'absolutely *safe* – I mean the state of mind in which one is inclined to say "I am safe, nothing can injure me whatever happens."'[4] Wittgenstein certainly did not have in mind the naive or superstitious belief that God will protect us from the ordinary dangers of accident, aggression, weakness and failure that are inseparable from human life. What he may have meant was something closer to what has been called a sense of 'ontological rootedness'[5] – a sense that, for all its difficulties and dangers, the world we inhabit is one in which we can feel ultimately at home.

Wittgenstein was not a religious believer, so there is a sense in which he was describing a promised land that he himself felt unable to enter. But it would be a major mistake to suppose that the initial entry point into the promised land has to be a purely doctrinal one – signing up to certain credal statements, for example. As already noted in our opening chapter, a vital part of entering the domain of religious belief has to do with praxis, with regular practical routines of religious observance. And it is this praxis that may be the key to nurturing the sense of rootedness without which life, however full of useful achievement, can seem ultimately flat and empty.

3

The human quest

> The soul is born to perceive the infinite good that is God
> and here alone can find rest.   (Bonaventure[1])

Human existence is difficult. Even for those in the developed world who enjoy unprecedented levels of comfort, life is hostage to the ever-present risks of accident, illness, depression, disappointment and failure. And even if we cheerily manage to forget all this, we can never entirely lose sight of the stark fact of our mortality. As the wry Woody Allen joke has it: 'You should live each day like it was your last – and one day you'll be right!'[2] Or to quote the old psychoanalytic jest: 'Doctor, doctor, I have a nameless fear.' 'Don't worry – we'll soon put a name to it!'

The existentialist philosophers had various names for this – 'angst', 'sickness-unto-death', 'fear and trembling', 'nausea'.[3] To be sure, there is plenty to be anxious about, and we all know what it is like to be racked by a specific worry – about one's job, perhaps, or an impending financial crisis, or the health of a loved one, so that the feeling one has when waking up in the morning is an all too familiar sickening lurch of fear: the ordeal continues, it still has to be faced, it has not gone away. But even when there is no particular preoccupation on the horizon, even when things seem 'normal' and comparatively comfortable, to be human is nevertheless to experience a certain residual *restlessness* – a characteristic sense of incompleteness.

The ancient Stoics spoke of happiness as involving a 'good flow of life'.[4] Their ideal was that of the philosophical sage whose life is characterized by a calmness, a mastery of the unruly passions, and an ordered progression of rationally ordered choices. But as Shakespeare pointedly observes, 'there was never yet philosopher who could endure the toothache patiently'.[5] However much we may want to pride ourselves on our intellectual detachment and rationality, we are not disembodied intellects, but vulnerable creatures of flesh and blood, and the resulting worries and insecurities to which we are prone affect us at much deeper levels than are accessed by the rational conscious mind.

Physical pain, or even chronic discomfort, can profoundly disrupt the 'good flow of life'. And mental anxieties can sap our energy and disturb our ability to think clearly and effectively pursue the tasks we have set ourselves. Perhaps one might imagine a scientific utopia in which the combined skills of the pharmacologist and the behavioural therapist could address the 'thousand natural shocks that flesh is heir to',[6] and alleviate all or most of our day-to-day ills. Yet one does not have to be an incurable pessimist to think that even in such a 'brave new world'[7] our residual human restlessness would never completely go away.

To be a religious believer is clearly not to have a magical cure for the anxiety that is inextricably bound up with the human condition. When St Augustine spoke of the 'unquiet heart', he was referring not to our intermittent oppression by specific cares, but to a more enduring aspect of the kind of creatures we are. To be a human is to be dependent, finite, not self-sufficient – and indeed this is a feature of our existence that no one, believer or not, could coherently deny. Yet for the believer, it is at the root of the religious impulse. For in the very fact of recognizing this weakness, this finitude, we are dimly aware of the infinite – the perfection we fall immeasurably short of, but to which we somehow aspire or towards which we yearn.

This line of reasoning owes something to Plato, and was further developed by the thirteenth-century Franciscan thinker St Bonaventure, only to reappear five centuries later in the *Meditations* of René Descartes.[8] Descartes is standardly considered to be the 'father of modern philosophy', the champion of cautious reasoning based on 'clear and distinct ideas'; but his reaching towards the infinite goes far beyond detached intellectual reflection. It involves a passionate encounter, characterized by awe and wonder, which dispels the darkness of doubt, and leads the meditator to 'gaze at, wonder at and adore the beauty of this immense light'.[9]

We are back with the importance of praxis. Descartes' meditator is not just thinking something, he is *doing* something, doubting: seeking, wondering, gazing, adoring. Augustine remarked that the 'restless heart' that is our human birthright could find rest and repose only in God.[10] And similarly for Descartes, the darkness and chaos that he plumbs when he resolves to doubt everything are dispelled only when he sees that in acknowledging his ignorance and weakness he is already implicitly acknowledging his creatureliness – the utter dependency of his finite being on the infinite light of truth and goodness that floods into his mind, 'in so far as the darkened intellect [of a finite creature] can bear it'.[11]

Philosophers will no doubt continue, as they have done for centuries, to analyse and debate the logic of Descartes' arguments. But a zeal for logical analysis, admirable though that may be, should not blind us to the practical effects of the encounter with the 'immense light' described in the *Meditations*. Descartes insisted that his arguments could not be properly assessed in a purely abstract and detached fashion: the only way to fully grasp them was for each of us, individually, to follow the meditator's path from doubt to affirmation.[12] And the hoped for results of the journey were not just to be a matter of theoretical or intellectual enlightenment, but to involve 'the greatest joy of which we are capable in this life'.[13]

How might undertaking such a journey affect the 'flow' of someone's life – not just the ordered progression of rational choices that Zeno and the Stoics had in mind, but the fundamental colour or tone of someone's existence? We have already spoken of the undercurrent of restlessness, the sense of incompleteness, that swirls close beneath the surface of our consciousness, always ready to bubble up and generate that characteristically human yearning for something greater in which our existence can be anchored – something that will secure our human existence and give it meaning. Undertaking the journey towards religious belief involves taking practical steps to find a *vehicle* for that yearning – a means whereby it can be transformed into a joyful and hopeful search whose flow and rhythm gives life meaning.

This is not a matter of final solutions. People often assume that definitive answers are precisely what the religious believer claims to possess, but the way many religious people talk about their experience suggests that being a believer is more like being engaged in a continuous quest than having reached a final destination. Nor can it even be said that the object of the search is fully and clearly in view. It is a fundamental postulate of mainstream Christianity, together with the other Abrahamic faiths, Judaism and Islam, that God is 'incomprehensible' – that is, incapable of being grasped or encompassed by the human mind.

Augustine warns against the blasphemy of thinking that God can be grasped – if you can grasp something, then that is the best evidence that it is not God but an idol of your own making.[14] We cannot grasp the infinite any more than we can put our arms round a mountain, Descartes observes, but we can reach towards it, and perhaps touch it.[15] To be a believer is to find a way of reaching towards the divine, so that instead of each day spent trying to distract ourselves and forget our ultimate precariousness and dependency, we affirm it, rejoicing in our finitude as that which points us towards something infinitely greater on which our ultimate peace depends.

4

Reaching for the unknown

I wonder at the existence of the world.
                    (Ludwig Wittgenstein[1])

How then do we reach towards that unknown, incomprehensible, infinite – the mysterious divine source of being without which, so classical theology maintains, everything would slip into nothingness?[2] If the question is posed in this way, it seems unanswerable: the problems and preoccupations of the ordinary natural and human world around us seem difficult enough without our having to grapple with metaphysical conundrums about the mystery of existence. And indeed the great German philosopher Immanuel Kant warned that if we leave the solid 'land of truth' (the ordinary world of the five senses) and venture out into the 'stormy ocean' of metaphysical speculation, we will be deluded with 'empty hopes', embarking on a voyage that we will 'be unable to abandon and yet unable to complete'.[3]

And yet the puzzle of existence is not just an 'academic' philosopher's puzzle. One does not have to be given to abstract speculative inquiry in order to be struck with a sense of wonder that there should be anything at all: 'How extraordinary that the world should exist!'[4] To be

14

sure, scientists can now give a convincing account of how the earth was formed, and the stars, and so on. But how there comes to be *anything at all*, why there is something rather than nothing, is an unanswerable mystery.

Traditionally, theologians have declared that God is the ultimate reason why the universe exists. Everything else is *contingent* – it depends on something else (for example, on some prior cause or set of causes). But God is taken to be 'necessary' – utterly independent and self-sufficient, containing within himself, as it were, the reason for his own existence. This kind of reasoning is one form of the so-called 'cosmological' argument for the existence of God.[5] And in its stress on the supreme reality and perfection of God it has something in common with another ancient argument for God, the 'ontological' argument, which proposes that since God is defined as the supremely perfect being – 'that than which nothing greater can be conceived' – he must necessarily exist (for if God were a fictitious entity existing only in the minds of theologians, he would be inferior to a real, independently existing God, and so not meet the definition of 'that than which nothing greater can be conceived').[6]

These and other classic arguments for God's existence, endlessly elaborated and refined, have fuelled centuries of heated discussion among philosophers. They are full of intellectual interest, but it is hard to suppose they are going to offer decisive help for someone who is wrestling with the question 'How can I believe?' Even if the arguments could be shown to be decisive (something few philosophers today would concede), they seem too abstract, too remote from our human predicament, to generate that radical moral and psychological change that turns someone into a religious believer.

'It is the heart, not reason, that senses God,' said Pascal in the seventeenth century.[7] This is sometimes interpreted to mean that religious faith is purely emotional, perhaps even irrational – which would make it a convenient target for the contemporary polemicists who allege that adopting a religious outlook involves abandoning proper scientific standards of evidence and proof. But Pascal's underlying point was a different one: that God is not the remote and abstract 'God of the philosophers',[8] not a God who reveals himself 'cold', as it were, to the detached spectator or sceptical inquirer, but one whose presence is felt by those who seek him earnestly, 'with all their heart'.[9]

For the great majority, becoming a believer is not going to be the conclusion of a philosophical argument. It will not depend on purely logical inference or empirical assessment, but, as suggested in the previous chapter, is intimately bound up with our anxious sense of human dependency and finitude, and our longing to find a home for the restless human heart. The God who would assuage this longing will not be a god who dwells apart in splendid isolation, perfectly self-sufficient, exempt from and indifferent to the nexus of causality in which all existing things are bound. Such a god could not be a god to whom the anxious heart reaches out with joy and hope. The God who answers to our need to believe will have to be a God who *seeks us out*, responding to something deep in our own nature that yearns, as St Paul put it, to 'seek him, and perhaps reach out for him and find him'.[10] For Paul, such a God, though remaining ultimately mysterious, dwelling in 'light inaccessible, whom no man hath seen or can see',[11] is nevertheless 'not far from any one of us, for in him we live and move and have our being'.[12]

So perhaps in addressing the question 'How can I believe?' it may be worth shifting our direction of gaze. Instead of poring over the intricate arguments for God's existence that philosophers and theologians have debated, we could begin closer to home, in the ordinary human world – the place where we 'live and move and have our being', and where Paul glimpsed the constant, close presence of the divine. From this perspective, so far from being an abstract, distant God, God is conceived of as *interior intimo meo*, as Augustine was later to put it, 'closer to me than I am to myself'.[13]

But can we really see the divine here? Looking at how humans behave in the world around us, and at the thoughts and desires that rise up within us, we find so much that is amiss. The all too familiar tendencies to arrogance, selfishness and callousness are quite enough to tell us that we are a flawed species, prone at best to constant lapses from the standards we know we should follow, and at worst to acts of unspeakable cruelty and violence. 'I see and approve the better course,' as the classical Roman poet Ovid bluntly put it, 'but I follow the worse.'[14] Yet our very ability to see and be dismayed by the dreadful flaws that mar our humanity shows that we also have within us something to measure them against. We know the good even as we turn away from it.

That, in essence, is the human predicament. But how does it help the path to religious belief? Could one not take a purely secular view of all this, and say that we humans are a mixture of virtuous and vicious impulses

– exactly what one would expect from a species that has learned to be violent and aggressive in the struggle to survive against fierce competitors, but has also learned the advantages of cooperation and gentleness within the family and the tribe? Why not just admit that human beings are 'to some degree a mess', as the British philosopher Bernard Williams once trenchantly put it? Why not say, with Williams, that as a result of our evolutionary past we are an 'ill-assorted bricolage of powers and instincts' – and that is all there is to it?[15] Why not just stop with this mixed picture, partly depressing, partly encouraging, that begins and ends with the natural biological and social world? Why bring God into the picture at all? To these crucial questions we will now turn.

5

The still small voice

Stern Daughter of the Voice of God . . .
Who art a light to guide, a rod
To check the erring and reprove . . .
From vain temptations dost set free
And calm'st the weary strife of frail humanity.

(William Wordsworth[1])

Our inherited human nature is a complex and often contradictory bundle of traits and capacities. So what is it among this ill-assorted mixture that speaks of the divine? A traditional religious answer points to the voice of conscience – the 'Stern Daughter of the Voice of God', as William Wordsworth graphically personified it in his 'Ode to Duty', whose opening lines appear above. It is striking that although we so often go astray we have a powerful sense that we could, and should, be doing better. And this sense of conscience is interpreted as directing us towards the divine – to something higher and greater than ourselves that we somehow aspire to follow, but repeatedly fall short of.

The secularist will say that there is nothing at all mysterious about our moral sense, certainly nothing that should lead us down the path to religious belief. When discussing the evolution of our moral sensibilities, Charles Darwin uses a highly significant phrase – the '*so-called* moral sense'.[2] His approach to conscience is, in essence, a deflationary one: this and other so-called 'higher' impulses, on his view, are merely natural feelings that have developed under selection pressure. So altruism and self-sacrifice (to take one example he discusses) may have arisen because tribes in which this trait is prominent would act selflessly in battle and hence 'be victorious over most other tribes, and this would be natural selection'.[3] For Darwin, our moral feelings are just like any other ingrained drives and inclinations – part of our natural, animal inheritance. There is nothing special, nothing specially exalted, about morality or about the conscience or moral sense that supposedly detects moral values. The entire phenomenon of morality is to be located as simply another part of the natural world.

This highly influential Darwinian account is presented within a framework of supposedly dispassionate scientific thinking, but it faces serious problems. For when we reflect on the domain of morality, it appears to involve something that differs in kind from anything found in the ordinary observable natural world. Moral values are not just more or less strong inclinations or propensities; they are, in the current philosophical jargon, 'normative' – that is to say, they exert an authoritative *demand* or *call* upon us, whether we like it or not.

To be sure, a certain tendency to kindness and compassion is to some degree a natural element in our make-up. But as Joseph Butler observed in the eighteenth century, it is equally true that other bad passions, such as anger, 'are themselves equally natural, and often most prevalent', and so it is plain that one set of passions, considered merely as natural, can no more be a law to us than the others.[4] If all we have is our mixture of inclinations, why, as it were, pin a gold star on one subset of them and regard it as authoritative? Where could such special authority come from?

One secularist response is to say that the special authority of the moral sense is illusory – a mere quirk of our psychological make-up. Sigmund Freud, writing about the same time as Darwin, suggested that the voice of conscience derives its aura of power from our childhood experience of the strict punitive control of the parent, which has been internalized into the psyche where it exerts a formidable hidden influence on our adult thinking.[5] But simply to say that the relevant feelings were implanted in us as children by our parents is only a very short-term explanation, since the question immediately arises as to how the relevant feelings were transmitted to them, when they were children, and so on indefinitely. And in any case, whatever their origins, feelings such as those of remorse and repentance, of being authoritatively called to account for what we do, are not easily written off as merely an unwanted residue from our childhood. On the contrary, most people would consider them to be an indispensable part of what it is to be a responsible adult.

In more recent times, secular philosophers have analysed the authoritative demands of morality in various naturalistic ways, arguing, for example, that they derive merely from existing social conventions, or from the goals we have decided to pursue, or from the rules that have been found to promote a certain kind of stable and flourishing society. But the trouble with all these solutions is that they make the demands of morality *conditional*: *if* we have these particular conventions or goals, then we have reason to follow these demands. Yet the essence of genuine moral demands – the requirement to be compassionate, for example – is that they remain incumbent upon us no matter what. We recognize that we ought to be compassionate even if social conventions change so that compassion is no longer expected of us. We recognize that we ought not to be cruel, even if we develop a taste for cruelty. Genuine ethical truths, like the wrongness of cruelty or the goodness of compassion, continue to hold good even if we don't like them, even if we turn against them, even if society's norms and conventions change.

The philosopher Immanuel Kant is famous for underlining this 'categorical' force, as he called it, of moral imperatives. But he maintained that they are a requirement of *reason*, and can be derived simply from considering what can rationally be willed or chosen.[6] Yet when Friedrich Nietzsche, writing a century later in his *Beyond Good and Evil*, extolled the 'superior' human being who would 'overturn eternal values' and learn to 'steel his heart against compassion', disturbing and repellent though we may find his proposal, it does not seem to violate any rational principle.[7] Nietzsche appears to have lacked the fundamental sense of shared human vulnerability that makes vivid the force of the commandment to 'do unto others as you would have them do unto you'.[8] But where does the force, the authority, of that commandment come from? The mere fact of human vulnerability does not explain it, nor the requirements of Kant's 'rational will'. To Nietzsche's *Übermensch*, convinced of the superiority of the strong creative spirit, it might be quite possible and rational to will that *he himself* should treated without pity should he be weak enough to fail in his grand projects.

In short, unless the whole idea of binding morality is an illusion, there appears to be something 'transcendent' about it: something that cannot be derived from the contingencies of mere biological drive or psychological inclination or social convention, and cannot be established simply by asking what can be 'rationally willed'.

However hard it is to explain, the fact remains that something deep within us, something that we call conscience, seems to be responsive to the binding requirements of morality. The pangs of conscience are felt within us, but they nonetheless present themselves as a response to something outside of us that somehow qualifies as objectively and independently authoritative.

The theistic view, as developed in Judaism, Christianity and Islam, affirms that our moral sense is a response to something quite independent of us – the God of justice and loving-kindness, as the Hebrew Bible says, or the God who is all-compassionate and all-merciful, as the Qur'an says, or the God who is identical with Love, as the Fourth Gospel says. Authentic objective moral value derives from the ultimate, eternal reality that is God.

One way of putting this traditional theistic view is to say that our minds, weak and finite though they are, possess an innate, divinely implanted intimation of eternal values. A partial parallel has been drawn here by a number of philosophers between our moral knowledge and our mathematical knowledge. René Descartes, for example, maintained that we can gain a basic insight, through the mathematical awareness implanted in us, of the laws that govern how the physical universe has to operate.[9] And somewhat similarly, he maintains that through the fundamental moral awareness implanted in us we have the power to discern how we ought to act, and to orient ourselves towards the good that lies at the heart of reality.[10] On this view, the strongest kind of objectivity is secured in the moral domain, just as it is in the domain of mathematical physics (though this need not, of course, mean that moral questions have quick and easy answers, any more than is the case in mathematics or science).

Even if one does not accept all the implications of such accounts of our mathematical and moral intuitions, these accounts seem to capture something important about the remarkable powers of the human mind. The contemporary American philosopher Thomas Nagel has spoken of the human mind as an 'instrument of transcendence that can grasp objective reality and objective value'.[11] Given today's largely secular philosophical climate, the phrase 'instrument of transcendence' is an amazing one for an analytic philosopher to use of the human mind. Yet Nagel is himself a declared atheist, and in calling the human mind an 'instrument of transcendence' he is not talking about immortal souls: he accepts that the relevant mental processes are inseparable from the physical processes of the body and brain. But the purely physical nature of these processes doesn't settle the question of what kind of reality our minds are responding to when we use our rational and moral capacities. And Nagel has the integrity to admit just how strange, from the point of view of modern materialist orthodoxy, that reality is. Our reason gives us access to an objective reality that somehow sustains the eternal and necessary truths of logic and mathematics, and the domain of objective, normative moral truth.

These remarkable facts may not prove the truth of theism; but they may reasonably be thought of as a pointer or a sign that cannot easily be discounted. For it seems that a world-view with God at its centre is fundamentally hospitable to the idea of genuinely objective normative standards like rationality and goodness, in a way that secular world-views are going to find it hard to be. In the Christian Scriptures, God is identified with reason or word (*logos*) and with love (*agape*) – attributes that are irreducibly personal.[12] So ultimate reality, on the God-centred view, is *personal* and *purposive*, rather than blind, irrational, neutral, random or blank (which is in the end what an alternative atheistical world-view must take it to be).[13] Our human grasp, albeit imperfect, of an objective domain of truth and goodness tells us that the cosmos we inhabit is one in which the theist – the believer in a personal God – can feel ultimately at home.

6

Intimations of the sacred

The face [of the other] opens the primordial discourse
whose first word is obligation.

(Emmanuel Levinas[1])

Can we really feel at home in the world? So much about
the universe we find ourselves thrown into is enigmatic,
and different people can plausibly form different inter-
pretations of its ultimate nature. Logic or science on their
own cannot definitively settle the dispute between theists
and atheists, or decide the question of which world-view
we ought to adopt. But the reflections in the previous
chapter may at least suggest that the theistic world-view
is not inherently unreasonable. On the contrary, it seems
strikingly consistent with our remarkable human ability
to grasp objective reality and objective value.

Yet for religious belief to be a live option, more seems
to be required than abstract reflection about the nature
and basis of moral value and objectivity. To be able to
trust that the world we inhabit is indeed ultimately rooted
in rationality and goodness, most of us will need to move
from the theoretical level to the practical or existential
level – to the domain of lived human experience.

But it turns out that philosophical theory and personal experience are here closely intertwined. For the 'normative' moral requirements discussed in the previous chapter seem to be directly manifested in our personal experience, whenever two human beings encounter one another. When the Good Samaritan came upon the robbed and injured traveller on the road down to Jericho, he did not *have* to help him – indeed, those who had come along the road before him had passed by on the other side.[2] Stopping to help may have been inconvenient, and it turned out to be expensive (if you undertake one commitment it tends to lead to another). But nevertheless the Samaritan felt the imperative, he heard the insistent and urgent call to be compassionate, just as everyone listening to the story is meant to hear it.

The twentieth-century Danish philosopher Knud Løgstrup may have been subconsciously influenced by this and other related parables when he spoke of the 'ethical demand' – something that has to be understood in the context of the vulnerability and need to trust others that is woven into the very fabric of human life.[3] There is an openness and responsiveness to another person that is morally required in any human encounter or relationship. Of course, we can ignore the demand – and all too often we do. But the 'face of the other' still confronts us, demanding our respect and compassion, condemning us if we ignore it.

In terms of the way it is experienced, this kind of moral demand is sometimes described in religious terms as having 'sacred' or 'holy' force.[4] The term 'sacred' has ancient connotations, but it signals something deserving of special respect or protection, something inviolable, resistant to the instrumental attitude that would treat everything and everyone as a mere means to an end, or a mere commodity to be used. This sense of the sacred, as Roger Scruton has persuasively argued, marks out a space set apart from the ordinary world of expediency and mutual self-interest; the demands of the sacred 'intrude from beyond the comfortable arena of our agreements'.[5]

Yet although the sacred 'intrudes', although it makes an 'inviolable' claim upon us, nevertheless as a matter of actual, brutal fact it can always be violated. We can and all too often do close our eyes to the humanity that shines out from the face of the other person. Yet the inviolable demand remains, and our own deepest experience testifies to our inability to shut it out or suppress it entirely.

Our powerful experience of the moral demands imposed on us in our encounters with fellow human beings is not the only instance (though it is perhaps the most important) where we have intimations of a 'transcendent' or 'sacred' dimension to our existence. Other examples include those profoundly moving and often morally transformative responses we have to the greatest works of the creative artist, in painting or poetry or music. And yet another example may be found in those 'spots of time', as Wordsworth calls them: moments of special intensity when we are overwhelmed by the power and beauty of the natural world, and seem to be taken beyond ourselves, transported into a dimension that discloses layers of meaning and value that were previously occluded.[6]

Great works of art can be despoiled and vandalized; the incomparable beauty of the natural world can be polluted and degraded; and the human being in distress can be callously ignored, or even treated with contempt and brutality. Such deliberate acts of desecration show that there is nothing in the call of the sacred that *compels* us to react, in the manner of a hurricane, say, or an earthquake. The reality we encounter in these vivid experiences of the sacred is not like a physical force. But for all that, it is a reality which we cannot in integrity deny.

In all these cases where we have vivid personal experience of what we have been calling a 'transcendent' or 'sacred' dimension to our existence, we seem to glimpse that reality amounts to more than the factual sequence of events mapped out by science. Reality is not exhausted by the realm of 'the facts' – what can be catalogued and measured and charted. True, we depend on this factual world – we could not exist without it. But in our intimations of the transcendent or the sacred, the world becomes *transfigured*: we see it as irradiated with meaning and value – a meaning and value that does not simply arise endogenously, as a mere subjective aspect of our thought, but reflects something not of our making to which we feel bound to respond.

Grasping this basic point is central to what it means to be a religious believer. It is often assumed – particularly by contemporary militant critics of religion – that the theist is above all a believer in 'supernatural' entities – some kind of strange, 'spooky' object or objects that are supposed to exist over and above the natural world. But this way of putting the matter can give a very misleading picture of what animates and motivates theistic belief.

Many centuries ago, Thomas Aquinas, one of the great philosophical architects of classical theism, was at pains to insist that God should not be thought of as an entity.[7] It is a form of idolatry to suppose that God is an additional item we can classify and list on top of those already identified.[8] For the theistic believer, God is the ultimate source, or that in which all things are 'grounded'. But to add that God is 'supernatural' is to add a kind of blank, a placeholder, which purports to inform but actually elucidates nothing.

'Nature', in any case, is itself a highly ambiguous term – one often used in a very restricted sense nowadays to refer to the empirical world as described via the language of science (thus the term 'naturalism' in contemporary philosophy generally implies a rejection of any reality not ultimately explicable in scientific terms). But Nature as commonly used in medieval and early-modern philosophy – Nature with a capital N, as it were – is a much richer notion, denoting, in the words of one classic philosophical text, 'nothing less than God himself or the ordered system of created things established by God'.[9] Nature in this sense is the natural world in which beauty and order are manifest; it is a *cosmos* in the strict etymological sense of the Greek term, a world shot through with meaning and value. To label God as 'supernatural' is to risk removing him from the very manifestation of the sacred here in the natural world that is one of our most important modes of access to the divine.[10]

The world is stranger than we had thought, richer than we had thought, more exacting than we had thought. For the believer, the divine mystery at its source is not another object to be added to those catalogued by the scientist. It is that which calls us to respond, to change, to orient our lives so that we are more able to hear the insistent call of the sacred, and to set about becoming the better selves that we have so far failed to be.

7

Evil and waste

The waste remains and kills.

(William Empson[1])

To see the world as manifesting 'beauty', 'order' and 'goodness', in the way that has been underlined so far, may call forth an obvious objection: what about all the ugliness in the world, the waste, the suffering, the cruelty? This, of course, is the time-honoured 'problem of evil' that many people take to be a decisive obstacle to belief in an all-powerful and benevolent God.

Many books, each many times the size of this slim volume, have been devoted to this problem. But it may nevertheless be worthwhile to mention some considerations that are sometimes overlooked that may affect just how decisive this supposed objection to theism really is.

First, a great deal of ugliness and waste in the world around us is clearly our own doing. Through long familiarity, we have perhaps ceased to be as aware as we should be of the nightmare we have created in much of the urban man-made world. Watching the crowd of people streaming over London Bridge, one of the speakers in T. S. Eliot's *The Waste Land* says he would never have supposed that 'death had undone so many'; the phrase recapitulates Dante's description of the lost souls in purgatory.[2] And when today we see the haunted faces imprisoned within the endless lines of traffic on our highways, the filthy poisonous waste that the vehicles belch out, the endless loads of refuse trucked out to landfill sites, the skies roaring day and night with planes full of grasping businesspeople, corrupt politicians and pampered tourists, the plastic-polluted oceans, the armaments factories bursting with ever more vicious means of killing and maiming people, we may well feel that we are witnessing the last days of humanity, and that a species such as ours no longer deserves to walk the earth.

But it cannot all be laid at our door. The misery brought about by the ravages of disease, not to mention 'natural causes' like earthquakes, floods and tornadoes, defies all calculation. Where, in the face of all this horrendous and undeserved suffering, is the supposedly all-powerful, all-benevolent God of classical theism?

Yet before we decide that this settles the matter, we need to recall that it is not as if the traditional theist has always thought that the world is a completely happy, jolly place, and then someone comes along and says, 'Oh, wait a minute – here's something you hadn't noticed – look at all this suffering!' The reality is that traditional theism has always had the keenest awareness of suffering right at its very centre. The most passionately spiritual and religious people in the world's history, the people who produced Moses and the prophets and Jesus and St Paul, were a people whose history was marked by the most terrible suffering – indeed, the constant threat of annihilation. This is the people whose Scriptures reflect endlessly on *chesed*, the loving-kindness of God.[3] So to come along and say that suffering is a decisive reason for abandoning traditional theism, as many secular philosophers do, seems far too quick a move. We need to look more deeply into how religious belief works before we are entitled to play that card.

In traditional theistic belief, God has never been thought of as a kind of Benthamite utilitarian who is supposed constantly to intervene in order to secure maximal comfort and happiness for the inhabitants of the planet.[4] The 'loving-kindness' or 'mercy' of God that figures so prominently in the Bible cannot be equated with the modern consequentialist-style desire for welfare maximization, but is inextricably bound up with an uncompromising insistence on righteousness and justice. The overriding imperatives enjoined by God in the Judaeo-Christian Scriptures are not utilitarian ones but moral ones, in the strong sense of duties, summed up in the paramount duty to love one's neighbour as oneself.[5]

We are so used to the consequentialist framework of our modern 'brave new world'[6] that it is sometimes difficult to think ourselves into this older biblical perspective. So consider the following question. What is the worst thing that can happen in your life? To suffer pain, to suffer horrible illness and disease, to be smashed up by a tornado or swept away by a tsunami? All these are, of course, terrible things, and they will probably be at the top of the list of bad things for those who think in utilitarian or consequentialist terms (as do many contemporary secular moralists). But the theistic answer is different: that acting unjustly or unrighteously – deliberately harming your neighbours, for instance, or failing to help them when in distress – is worse, *infinitely worse*, than yourself undergoing pain or distress, or even death. It is infinitely worse to do evil than to suffer evil.[7]

To believe in God is not to be able to explain why terrible things happen, and why many lives are ruined or tragically cut short. The message of the book of Job is absolutely clear on this point: there is no explanation, or no explanation we can comprehend. To be a believer is not to 'solve' this problem, but is something else entirely. It is to hold that the meaning and purpose of our lives, for as long as it is granted to us to exist, is to live in accordance with the 'sacred' requirements of justice and compassion. To believe in God, as the theist understands it, is to believe that we are required, by a holy and inviolable power not of ourselves, to do what is right and to avoid what is wrong. And the world we inhabit, and the lives we have been given, are manifestly such as to allow us to do just that.

8

Belief and observance

Denken ist danken. (To think is to thank.)
(Seventeenth-century Pietist slogan[1])

So where, as our discussion draws to a close, have we arrived? If the reasoning outlined in this book is at all plausible, there need be no insuperable theoretical or philosophical problem in the way of becoming a believer. On the contrary, the idea of God, of the divine, the sacred, the holy, accords with some of our deepest human intuitions. In our experience of the unalterable requirements of justice and compassion, in our responses to the overwhelming beauties of nature and to the spiritually transformative power of great art and music, we humans seem to encounter a sacred or transcendent dimension to our existence. In all these cases, the reality that we encounter is one that can quite properly and reasonably be understood in terms of a theistic framework.

So if a 'problem' remains about becoming a believer, it seems that it is not so much at the theoretical level but at the practical one – at the level of what people often call 'spirituality'. What practical steps can we take to orient our lives so as to respond to the call of the sacred, and to grow in knowledge and love of the good?

It is plain that we cannot set about the task on our own. Enough has been said about the weakness and the vulnerability of the human condition for us to be sure that it would be difficult or impossible to try to devise a system of spiritual praxis from scratch. We are not wholly autonomous and self-sufficient beings; we cannot be 'epistemic egoists'.[2] We need the help of established routines of observance, structures of attentiveness and humility that will give rhythm and shape to our search.

We learn by doing. And by adopting the frameworks of spiritual practice that have come down to us in the various traditions, including prayer, meditation, alms-giving, self-examination and so on, the hope is that we can reinforce our sense of the sacred, make space for greater self-awareness, and develop a keener sensitivity to the needs of others. There is nothing new in all this: the point is simply that we cannot make progress just by an act of will, however worthy. Just as in the case of a schoolchild, or an athlete, or a musician, what is eventually achieved will depend in large part on systematic habituation and careful training. Becoming a religious believer will not be an isolated mental act, but a long process of growth.

But which specific religious framework are we talking about? It will not have escaped the reader that quite a lot of the thinking in previous chapters has been impli-citly informed by a theistic framework of the Judaeo-Christian kind, which is also shared by Islam. The central idea in all the Abrahamic faiths is, of course, that of a personal God, of supreme power and moral perfection, source of all reality and goodness.

Yet there are other frameworks – polytheistic ones, for example, as in Hinduism, not to mention atheistic forms of religion, as in Buddhism, where reality is not conceived in personal terms at all but as an impersonal flux of conditions that arise and pass away. And the very plurality of religions on the planet has been used by many modern critics of religion as a supposedly decisive argument against the reasonableness of being a religious believer – an approach that goes back at least to John Stuart Mill in the nineteenth century, when he acidly observed that 'the same causes which make [someone] a churchman in London would have made him a Buddhist or a Confucian in Peking'.[3]

The reflective believer will inevitably be all too aware that if he or she had been born in another period of history, or another geographical region, his or her religious allegiance would very likely have been quite different. So how can the specific commitment and allegiance that is necessary for religious belief to flourish be combined with a respect for different but equally powerful commitments expressed in divergent faiths – commitments that one recognizes could very well have been one's own had things been different?

An initial answer might be attempted by way of analogy. There is no contradiction in being wholeheartedly committed to one's spouse while recognizing that, had the accidents of personal history or geography been different, one might have married someone else. What is more, though marriages may take many divergent forms, these forms may all be thought of as responses to a universal human need. Without labouring the comparison, somewhat analogous points could reasonably be made about religious commitment.

But the analogy seems to break down in one crucial respect. Unlike the marriage case, it seems essential for religious commitment that one believes one's own religion to represent the ultimate objective truth about the universe. Yet given that the teachings of all the different religions contradict each other, they obviously cannot all be true. So what could possibly justify the insistence that this one specific variety of religious belief is the true one, while so many others must be false?

This last question may be an unsettling one, but on reflection it does not amount to the knock-down objection to religious belief that it is often taken to be. It is true that one can find many religious adherents who make stridently exclusivist claims, proclaiming that their beliefs alone represent knowledge of the final and ultimate truth. But given our human finitude and our cognitive limitations, it seems more appropriate for reflective religious believers to characterize their outlook in more tentative terms, as a search, a reaching forward to the divine.

Such a reaching forward will no doubt have to be based on something in our human cognitive apparatus that we believe gives us glimpses or intimations of the divine. But it will not need to insist on being definitive knowledge of the complete and final truth. Even St Paul, not perhaps best known for being tentative, and who expressed complete confidence that in Christ he had glimpsed the 'image of the invisible God',[4] was nevertheless fully ready to accept that there are limits to what we can know: 'now we see through a glass, darkly'.[5]

Mention of our human finitude brings us back finally to a theme that has recurred throughout our discussion. Given the weakness of our nature, and how very much we know we have still to learn about the universe we live in, it may seem hard or even absurd to stand up and say

'I believe . . .', especially when what is at stake is nothing less than the ultimate nature of reality and the ultimate meaning of our lives.

But this much we do know. In the very fact of being aware of our limits, of our finitude, we are implicitly reaching forward to the infinite. To be human is to have transcendent aspirations. In the ancient words of the Psalm, 'Like as the hart desireth the water brooks, so longeth my soul after thee, O God.'[6] We cannot wish that longing away. Even if science were to offer a complete map of reality and establish that the entire universe is finite, we would still have the ineradicable human yearning to know more, to reach beyond the boundaries that have been set, to seek for a perfection we know we fall short of.[7]

In the moral sphere, above all, we yearn to transcend our wretchedness and failure – to reduce, if only infinitesimally, the gap between what we are and what we aspire to be. As we struggle forward, we have a powerful sense that this transcendent yearning for the good is not merely a strange endogenous quirk of our biology or psychology, but is a response to something authoritative that transcends our own private inclinations and the conventions and rules of our society. The call of justice and righteousness and compassion is one that we hear, even when we stop our ears to it. And however much we resist it, it has an authority that we cannot in integrity deny.

To be a believer is to find a way of enacting these truths, in our daily and weekly lives, by adopting patterns of religious observance that help us along the necessary path to change. Religions are human institutions, all of them flawed, and when added to the flaws we ourselves bring to them, we know that there are risks in giving our allegiance, and that there are no guarantees. But in every enterprise of momentous human significance there are risks. If we only walked the path tested and certified in advance by the established methods of science (immensely valuable though those methods are), our lives would be radically impoverished.

Commitment is a form of love, and if the basic premise of theistic belief is true, the God to whom the believer entrusts his or her life is a God of love.[8] To ask 'How can I believe?' is, in a way, like asking 'How can I love?' And the only adequate answer to this question will take me beyond myself towards trust in the Other who calls forth that love. Such an answer makes me dependent on another – but that is what it is to be human in the first place. The only choice we have as human beings is whether to remain closed in on ourselves in a fantasy of human autonomy and self-sufficiency, or to reach out beyond ourselves in thankfulness and love.

Notes

The argument of this book aims to be self-standing, and does not presuppose any philosophical expertise, or acquaintance with the texts cited here. The references given below simply identify the passages quoted or alluded to in the text. They may also be of use to any readers interested in looking at some of the classic philosophical texts that have influenced our understanding of religious belief, as well as some contemporary philosophical contributions to the debate about religion.

1 The starting point

1 Evelyn Waugh, *Brideshead Revisited* (London: Chapman and Hall, 1945), Part I, Ch. 4.
2 See Charles Taylor, *A Secular Age* (Cambridge, MA: Harvard University Press, 2007), Introduction.
3 Sam Harris <www.samharris.org/blog/item/the-problem-with-atheism> (accessed May 2016). See also Harris, *Waking Up: A Guide to Spirituality Without Religion* (New York: Simon and Schuster, 2014).
4 Christopher Hitchens, in debate with Tony Blair (2010); text available at <http://monicks.net/2010/11/27/christopher-hitchens-vs-tony-blair-the-full-transcript/> (accessed May 2016).

2 Why want to believe in the first place?

1 Blaise Pascal, *Pensées* (*c.*1660), ed. L. Lafuma (Paris: Seuil, 1962), no. 418. An English edition is available by A. J. Krailsheimer (Harmondsworth: Penguin, 1966).

2 See Pascal's famous 'wager', *Pensées*, no. 418.

3 John 10.10.

4 Ludwig Wittgenstein, *A Lecture on Ethics* (1929), in *Philosophical Review* (1965), p. 8. Online at <www.geocities.jp/mickindex/wittgenstein/witt_lec_et_en.html> (accessed June 2016).

5 Simon May, *Love: A History* (New Haven, CT: Yale University Press, 2011), p. 7.

3 The human quest

1 St Bonaventure, *Commentaries on the Sentences of Peter Lombard* [*Commentarii Sententiarum Petri Lombardi*, 1248–55], I, 1, iii, 2, in *Opera Omnia* (Collegium S. Bonaventurae: Quarachhi, 1891), I, 40. The theme appears earlier, for example in St Augustine, *Confessions* [*Confessiones*, *c*.398], Bk I.

2 In the Woody Allen film *Café Society* (2016).

3 For the first three, see Søren Kierkegaard, *The Concept of Anxiety* [*Begrebet Angest*, 1844]; *Fear and Trembling* [*Frygt og Bæven*, 1843]; *The Sickness Unto Death* [*Sygdommen til Døden*, 1849]; transl. in H. V. and E. H. Hong, *The Essential Kierkegaard* (Princeton, NJ: Princeton University Press, 1995). See also J. Chamberlain and J. Rée (eds), *The Kierkegaard Reader* (Oxford: Blackwell, 2001). For nausea, see Jean-Paul Sartre's novel, *La Nausée* (1938), transl. R. Baldick (London: Penguin, 2000).

4 The phrase is attributed to Zeno of Citium (335–263 BC), the founder of Stoicism. See A. A. Long and D. N. Sedley (eds), *The Hellenistic Philosophers* (Cambridge: Cambridge University Press, 1987), no. 63A & B.

5 William Shakespeare, *Much Ado About Nothing* (1598), Act V, scene 2.

6 William Shakespeare, *Hamlet* (*c*.1601), Act III, scene 1.

7 Aldous Huxley's *Brave New World* (1931) brilliantly satirizes the idea that genetic engineering, behavioural conditioning and pharmacological intervention could eradicate all the ills of the human condition.

8 St Bonaventure, *Journey of the Mind Towards God* [*Itinerarium mentis in Deum*, 1259], III, 3; René Descartes, *Meditations* [*Meditationes de prima philosophia*, 1641], Third Meditation.

9 Descartes, Third Meditation, final paragraph.

10 Augustine, *Confessions*, Book I, Ch. 1.

11 Descartes, Third Meditation, final paragraph.

12 Descartes, *Meditations*, Preface to the Reader.

13 Descartes, Third Meditation, final sentence.

14 Augustine, *Sermons* [*Sermones*] 52:16 (early fifth century); available at <www.ewtn.com/library/PATRISTC/PNI6-5.TXT>.

15 Descartes, Letter to Mersenne of 27 May 1630. Translations of this and all texts of Descartes referred to may be found in J. Cottingham, R. Stoothoff and D. Murdoch (eds), *The Philosophical Writings of Descartes*, vols I and II (Cambridge: Cambridge University Press, 1985), and vol. III, The Correspondence, by the same translators plus A. Kenny (Cambridge: Cambridge University Press, 1991).

4 Reaching for the unknown

1 Ludwig Wittgenstein, *A Lecture on Ethics* (1929), in *Philosophical Review* (1965), p. 8. Online at <www.geocities.jp/mick index/wittgenstein/witt_lec_et_en.html> (accessed June 2016).

2 Thomas Aquinas, *Summa theologiae* (1266–73), Part I, question 9, article 2.

3 Immanuel Kant, *Critique of Pure Reason* [*Kritik der reinen Vernunft*, 1781/1787], A235/B294.

4 Wittgenstein, *Lecture on Ethics*.

5 See the third of Aquinas's 'Five Ways'; *Summa theologiae*, Part I, Question 2, article 3. See also Gottfried Leibniz, 'On the Radical Origination of Things' ['De rerum originatione radicali', 1697], translated in G. H. R. Parkinson (ed.), *Leibniz: Philosophical Writings* (London: Dent, 1973), pp. 137–44.

6 Anselm, *Proslogion* (1077), Ch. 3; compare Descartes, *Meditations* [*Meditationes de prima philosophia*, 1641], Fifth Meditation.

7 Blaise Pascal, *Pensées* (*c.*1660), ed. L. Lafuma (Paris: Seuil, 1962), no. 424.
8 Pascal, *Pensées*, no. 913.
9 Pascal, *Pensées*, no. 427.
10 Acts 17.27.
11 1 Timothy 6.16.
12 Acts 17.28.
13 Augustine, *Confessions*, Bk III, Ch. 6, §11.
14 '*Video meliora proboque, deteriora sequor*'; Ovid, *Metamorphoses* (AD 8), Bk VII, line 20.
15 Bernard Williams, 'Replies', in J. Altham and R. Harrison (eds), *World, Mind, and Ethics* (Cambridge: Cambridge University Press, 1995), p. 199.

5 The still small voice

1 William Wordsworth, 'Ode to Duty' (1805).
2 Charles Darwin, *The Descent of Man* (1871), Ch. 4.
3 Darwin, *Descent of Man*, Ch. 5.
4 Joseph Butler, *Fifteen Sermons* (1726), Sermon II, §8.
5 Sigmund Freud, *Civilization and its Discontents* [*Das Unbehagen in der Kultur*, 1929], Ch. 7.
6 Immanuel Kant, *Groundwork for the Metaphysic of Morals* [*Grundlegung zur Metaphysik der Sitten*, 1785], transl. and ed. T. E. Hill and A. Zwieg (Oxford: Oxford University Press, 2002), Section 2.
7 Friedrich Nietzsche, *Beyond Good and Evil* [*Jenseits von Gut und Böse*, 1886], §37.
8 Matthew 7.12.
9 See Descartes, *Discourse on the Method* [*Discours de la méthode*, 1637], Ch. 5.
10 For Descartes, our will spontaneously follows the 'great light' in the intellect which discloses 'reasons of truth and goodness'; see Descartes, *Meditations* [*Meditationes de prima philosophia*, 1641], Fourth Meditation.
11 Thomas Nagel, *Mind and Cosmos* (Oxford: Oxford University Press, 2012), p. 85.

12 John 1.1; 1 John 4.8.

13 For an attempt to preserve purposiveness in the cosmos without God (or at any rate without the kind of God envisaged in traditional theism), see Tim Mulgan, *Purpose in the Universe* (Oxford: Oxford University Press, 2015).

6 Intimations of the sacred

1 '*Le visage ouvre le discours original dont le premier mot est obligation*'; Emmanuel Levinas, *Totality and Infinity* [*Totalité et Infini*, 1961], trans. A. Lingis (Dordrecht: Kluwer, 1991), III, B, 2.

2 Luke 10.25–37.

3 Knud Løgstrup, *The Ethical Demand* [*Den Etiske Fordring*, 1956], eds H. Fink and A. MacIntyre (Notre Dame, IL: University of Notre Dame Press, 1997).

4 Levinas, for various reasons, mistrusts the term 'sacred' and prefers 'holy'; see John Caruana, '"Not Ethics, Not Ethics Alone, but the Holy": Levinas on Ethics and Holiness', *Journal of Religious Ethics*, Vol. 34 (2006), pp. 561–83.

5 Roger Scruton, *Beyond Human Nature* (Princeton, NJ: Princeton University Press, 2017), p. 116.

6 William Wordsworth, *The Prelude*, Book 12, lines 208–18 (1805 edition). See also John Cottingham, 'Human Nature and the Transcendent', in Constantine Sandis and M. J. Cain (eds), *Human Nature*, Royal Institute of Philosophy supplement 70 (Cambridge: Cambridge University Press, 2012), pp. 233–54.

7 Thomas Aquinas, *Commentary on Aristotle's Peri Hermeneias* [*Sententiae super Peri Hermeneias*, 1270–71].

8 See Rupert Shortt, *God is No Thing* (London: Hurst, 2016).

9 René Descartes, *Meditations* [*Meditationes de prima philosophia*, 1641], Sixth Meditation.

10 For a fascinating discussion of scientific 'naturalism' in contemporary philosophy, and the possibility of a richer naturalism that accommodates belief in God, see Fiona Ellis, *God, Value, and Nature* (Oxford: Oxford University Press, 2014).

7 Evil and waste

1 William Empson, 'The Missing Dates' (1937) in Empson, *The Complete Poems* (London: Penguin, 2001).

2 T. S. Eliot, *The Waste Land* (1922), Part I, line 62; compare Dante, *The Divine Comedy: Inferno* [*La Divina Comedia: Inferno, c.*1310], III, 55–7.

3 See further John Cottingham, *The Spiritual Dimension* (Cambridge: Cambridge University Press, 2005), Ch. 2, §2.

4 Jeremy Bentham, founder of the utilitarian ethics that has so influenced our modern culture, declared the fundamental basis of morality to be 'the greatest happiness of the greatest number'; *An Introduction to the Principles of Morals and Legislation* (1789).

5 Leviticus 19.17; Mark 12.32–33.

6 See above, Chapter 3, note 7.

7 A principle that was also recognized by Socrates, several centuries before Christ; see *Plato, Gorgias* (*c.*380 BC), 469a–479e.

8 Belief and observance

1 The slogan is made use of by Martin Heidegger, in *What Do We Mean By Thinking?* [*Was Heisst Denken?*, 1954].

2 See Linda Zagzebski, *Epistemic Authority* (Oxford: Oxford University Press, 2012), Chs 1 and 2.

3 John Stuart Mill, *On Liberty* (1859), Ch. 2.

4 Colossians 1.15.

5 1 Corinthians 13.12.

6 Psalm 42.1.

7 Adrian Moore, 'A History of the Infinite', broadcast on BBC Radio Four in 2016, and available as a podcast at <www.bbc.co.uk/programmes/b07wr1lz>.

8 1 John 4.10: 'This is love, not that we love God, but that he first loved us.'